table of con[tents]

tools to use

Tim shares his original techniques plus popular papers and accessories to inspire creativity. Enjoy your creative journey...

distress ink™

Tim Holtz Distress Inks from Ranger are water-based dye inks specially formulated to create an aged look on papers, photos, and are PERFECT for distressables. The inks blend and shade on the papers and doo-dads with vintage tones to give you the look you want. For the metal accents, Tim Holtz Adirondack Alcohol Inks from Ranger will transform plain metals into colorful accents.

scissors

It is very important to choose the right kind of scissors when you are trying to cut out the distressable doo-dads. The heavyweight board requires a detailed tip to cut out exactly what you want without leaving a path of scissor destruction. My favorite is from Tonic Studios #814. Its detailed tip and serrated edge make all the difference when cutting out tiny images.

adhesives

I know we all have our personal favorites when it comes to adhesives. Are you a glue person or a tape person? Well, whatever your choice is, here is some advice on choosing the right one for the job. First, glue pens work the best for the tiny things while glue sticks are great for a quick stick. Heavier craft glues like The Ultimate! or Glossy Accents will come in handy for mica and other heavier embellishments. Double-sided foam tapes are just what you need to add a little dimension to your work.

sanding block

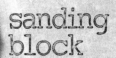

One of my favorite things about distressables is that they can all be sanded. Whether your preference is fine grit to heavy grit, you'll be sure to get the results you're looking for. My tool of choice is the Scrapper's Block which is a double-sided two-grit foam sanding block that won't damage your hands when working with tiny doo-dads or large papers, and it's just the right amount of sanding to get ready for ink.

ink applicators

The trick to getting ink on your projects just the right way is using the right ink applicator. Cut n' Dry Foam is a durable foam pad that can be cut to any size to get ink even in the smallest areas of your projects. Sponges, brushes and other craft tools can also be used. Take time to experiment.

punches

The distressables doo-dads line is sized so you can use your favorite punches with them. Whether it's a hand punch or thumb-punch, the right one is available in the size you need. Of course, you can still cut the images any shape you choose.

Now that you have the right tools for creative success, let's get started on the basics...

basics

These basic techniques are the general how-to's when working with distressables that will be referenced throughout the book. Of course, these are just the basics, as I am sure you'll take these products on a whole creative journey of your own.

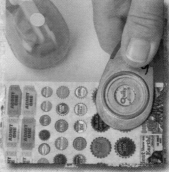

cutting

The first thing you'll have to embrace is the fact that distressables doo-dads are designed for you to cut up. So break out those scissors and remember these few tips:

It's much easier and there is less chance of waste if you cut your doo-dads strips across first instead of trying to work "the maze" to get what you want. Trust me.

When cutting your images, leave about 1/8" edge to sand. Too much of a border detracts from the image.

Watch your fingers! These tiny doo-dads are sometimes tricky to hold on to. Just make sure of what you are cutting.

Again, the right scissors make all the difference.

sanding

The next step is to sand your work. C'mon it's fun. Give it a try! Play with different grits and tools, but keep these things in mind:

Sand the edges working from top to bottom – not left to right. This will give you a better distressed edge for inking.

You don't need to sand too hard. Remember distressables were designed to sand. You'll see what I mean.

I have found that the lighter grit is easier on your hands. You still have to hold on to these things.

punching

You're going to love the fact that the distressables doo-dads are designed to be used with your punches. This sure removes the agony of cutting tiny circles. Here are some ideas to make punching a little easier:

Flip your punch over and look at what you're punching out. Pretty neat, huh?

Keep an eye on the image. They tend to fly across the room if you're not careful.

A standard hand-held hole punch is perfect for the typewriter keys. Other sizes of circles are available at most craft stores too.

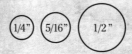

inking

By far my favorite thing to do! Of course, distressables will need some Distress Ink! Use whatever colors you want to achieve the look you desire. Most of my projects use Vintage Photo or Walnut Stain, but occasionally Black Soot. Distress Inks will definitely make all the difference in your finished distressables creations. Here are some things to keep in mind:

Apply the Distress Inks with Cut n' Dry Foam or even a sponge. Be careful if you go direct from the pad because the inks can get dark.

Distress Inks are formulated to react with water so your inked papers will give you instant vintage looking papers.

Add ink to EVERYTHING. It not only adds depth to your work, but a finished look as well.

5262

Tim Holtz distressables

fabulous techniques for ...

aging
distressing
layering
patinas
collage
soldering
transfers
folding
painting
scratching
glazing
and more!

create your own terrific...

cards
jewelry
accessories
scrapbooks
& more!

Design Originals

No. 5262

Design Originals

Tim Holtz distressables

As a well-known designer, Tim Holtz has been a frequent guest on HGTV's The Carol Duvall Show and his projects can be seen regularly in books and magazines.

This fabulous book is filled with Tim's original techniques and tips that are creative and inspiring for crafters and beyond...

Tim is the Designer and Senior Educator for Ranger Industries – one of the leading manufacturers of innovative inks, embossing and craft products.

He is involved in product development and one of his signature lines of products includes Distress Inks and distressables papers.

Tim travels internationally to trade shows and stores to educate and introduce people to his world of inks and so much more...

For a color catalog featuring over 200 terrific 'How-To' books, send $3.00 to **CATALOG**, Design Originals, Dept. C-1, 2425 Cullen St, Ft Worth, TX 76107 **or visit www.d-originals.com**

This valuable book contains terrific techniques and secrets to guide you on your creative journey. It features the Tim Holtz signature line of distressable papers and doo-dad embellishments. Designed especially for you, the paper crafter, who is looking for a little something different, this line includes fun things to use... from distressable papers to doo-dads, from cutable strips to mini folders, from slide mounts to metal accents. The Tim Holtz Collection has everything you need to create incredible paper craft projects.

The vintage images and colors of papers are perfect for layering and allow you to take total control of your layout or project. Coordinating doo-dads are cutable, punchable, sandable, and most of all, distressable using Tim Holtz Distress Inks from Ranger. Add the metal accents to create a dimensional look for jewelry, scrapbook pages, cards and more. The miniature images allow you to collage on dominoes, slide mounts, bottle caps and other tiny trinkets... the possibilities are endless.

Enjoy your creative journey into a world where our memories and artistic dreams are often larger than life itself...

Tim

alcohol ink

Another favorite of mine because it is ink too, of course! Adirondack Alcohol Inks are a perfect way to alter metal accents like mini clips, bottle caps, and more. These translucent colored inks work on all non-porous surfaces. Here is what you need to know to apply them to your projects:

Make sure your surface is clean from oils, lotions, etc.

Apply Alcohol Inks to a felt ink applicator or use your Cut n' Dry for this too.

Tap the ink directly on your surface and watch the magic happen. The colors blend and mix right before your eyes.

Alcohol Inks dry quickly, but you can speed it up using your heat tool.

If your colors are too intense or you want to change them altogether, add some Adirondack Blending Solution to your applicator and it will lighten, blend and even remove colors.

layering

The basic thing to remember when layering is that you are trying to create the illusion of depth. Everyone has their own thoughts about layering, mine would be - less is more, and it's all about the ink!

When layering, start with your background first. Use collage papers, ink, paints, or any other media to create the basic background.

Like I said, it's all about the ink. Any layer added to the background can be dimensionalized with a little ink – Distress Ink, that is. This will create a shadow look around the image you are layering.

Foam tapes, glue dots, and other dimensional adhesives are also a great way to add height and shadow to your inked image.

When assembling your layers, overlapping images and sometimes having an object "bleed" off the background will provide even more depth.

patinas

Sometimes we need to add an aged look to metal accents like our great mini-clips, chain, or even foil tape. My suggestion is Black Patina that you can find at most stained glass stores. This is much easier to work with. It has less smell, it's safer, and faster.

I simply apply it using a cotton swab and the results are instant and aged. ***Do not get it near any metal that you do not want to age, such as jewelry, scissors, etc.

Next, wipe off the solution with a wet cloth or paper towel to stop the process.

That's it! No sealers or anything.

scoring & folding

A fold is just a fold – right? Well not exactly. With some simple tips you will be a folding genius with successful results every time. Here are some things to keep in mind:

As always, having the right tools for the job is a must. A bone folder is key here.

To score a fold, place a ruler or straight edge along where you would like the fold to be. Then slightly press the bone folder against the straight edge and "score" the paper.

Using the score mark, fold the paper OPPOSITE of the score mark. In other words, when you score the paper, you put a groove into the paper. Fold it so the groove is on the outside of the fold.

Finally, crease the folded paper using the bone folder to assure a clean, pressed, and professional fold. This will make your paper projects perfect!

Capture your timeless memories in a timepiece. Special moments in your life can be expressed with images, words and the elements of time...

elements of time
dimensional collage

1. Create a template by tracing the back of the watch body. Cut it out inside the lines, making sure the piece fits inside the watch back.

2. Place the template on background paper. Trace the template and cut it out.

3. Cut out the doo-dads images. Sand and ink the edges.

4. Adhere doodads to the background with foam tape.

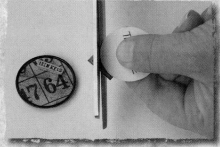

5. Trim off any excess images to fit the original template size.

6. Glue a dimensional object on the background making sure the object height will fit inside the closed watch.

7. Place the completed background into the watch back and add watch parts without gluing. The parts are free to move.

8. Place the watch top on the background and tap closed with a rubber mallet.

how to: see page 7.

Journey Watch Case
Finished size: 1 1/2"

Supplies:
- Design Originals (distressables cardstock #0743 Rulers; doo-dads #0755 Dark Words, #0754 Typewriter)
- Ranger (Distress Ink, Cut n' Dry foam pad)
- Watch (Body, Parts)
- Pen nib
- Ball chain
- Scissors
- Sanding block
- Crafter's Pick The Ultimate! glue
- Double stick foam tape
- Glue stick

Bingo Trinkets Watch Case
Finished size: 1 1/2"

Supplies:
- Design Originals (distress-ables cardstock #0738 Bingo; doo-dads #0755 Dark Words)
- Ranger (Distress Ink, Cut n' Dry foam pad)
- Watch (Body, Parts)
- Game piece
- Ball chain
- Scissors
- Sanding block
- Crafter's Pick The Ultimate! glue
- Double stick foam tape
- Glue stick

Question Time Watch Case
Finished size: 1 1/2"

Supplies:
- Design Originals (distressables cardstock #0733 Time; doo-dads: #0755 Dark Words, #0756 Light Words, #752 Print Blocks, #0754 Typewriter)
- Watch (Body, Parts)
- Ball chain
- Scissors
- Sanding block
- Double stick foam tape
- Glue stick

how to:
see page 7.

tips & tricks

Create personalized watches for birthdays, anniversaries and graduations using photographs.

*

For a baby keepsake, add a mini photo or mini birth announcement, birth date, and a lock of hair.

*

For a wedding favor, add a mini announcement, wedding date, and some birdseed or rice.

*

Use these timepieces on books, or framed shadowboxes.

*

Create a key chain instead of a pendant by adding a key ring to a jump ring.

* * * * *

trinkets of tin
laminating with mica

Travel Postale Keepsake Tin
Finished size:
1" x 1 7/8"

Supplies

- Design Originals (distress-ables cardstock #0737 Postale; doo-dads #0756 Light Words; #1943 Silver Metal Clip)
- Ranger (Distress Ink, Cut n' Dry foam pad)
- Mica
- Small sliding mint tin
- Charm
- Ball chain
- Scissors
- Sanding block
- Crafter's Pick The Ultimate! glue
- Double stick foam tape
- Glue stick

Create a work of art from a simple tin. Layer images, word and trinkets on this wearable treasure with a hidden place to keep your secrets in...

how to: see page 11.

1. Create a template for the small slide tin.

2. Place templates on background paper. Trace templates and cut out.

INSIDE
TEMPLATE

3. Ink the edges of the top background. Glue the background to lid of the tin.

4. Glue a mica tile over the background. Let dry. Trim off excess.

TOP
TEMPLATE

5. Cut out doo-dads. Sand and ink the edges. Adhere to the background with foam tape.

6. Ink the edges of the inside background. Glue it inside the tin.

Life Time Keepsake Tin
Finished size: 1" x 1 7/8"

Supplies:
- Design Originals (distressables cardstock #0734 Print Blocks; doo-dads: #0756 Light Words, #0754 Typewriter, #1943 Silver Metal Clip)
- Ranger (Distress Ink, Glossy Accents, Cut n' Dry foam pad)
- Mica
- Small sliding mint tin
- Watch
- Ball chain
- Scissors
- Sanding block
- Crafter's Pick The Ultimate! glue
- Double stick foam tape
- Glue stick

how to:
see page 11.

Remember When Keepsake Tin
Finished size: 1" x 1 7/8"

Supplies:
- Design Originals (distressables cardstock #0738 Bingo, #0737 Postale, #0743 Rulers; doo-dads #0756 Light Words, #1943 Silver Metal Clip)
- Ranger (Distress Ink, Cut n' Dry foam pad)
- Mica
- Small sliding mint tin
- Charm
- Ball chain
- Scissors
- Sanding block
- Crafter's Pick The Ultimate! glue
- Double stick foam tape
- Glue stick

Fill tin with a tiny accordion book, domino art, mirror, or other tiny collectibles.

*

Glaze finished tin with Ultra Thick Embossing Enamel instead of mica for a glazed look:

1. Ink background with clear embossing ink.
2. Apply clear UTEE.
3. Heat with Heat Tool until melted.
4. Apply additional layers of UTEE while hot and continue to melt with Heat Tool.

*

Drill a hole in the bottom of the tin to add wire and charms.

*

Add a clip to the tin top. Secure with glue or solder.

* * *

how to:
see page 11.

Admit One Keepsake Tin
Finished size 1 3/8" x 3 1/4"

Supplies:
- Design Originals (distressables cardstock #0741 Circus, #0737 Postale; doo-dads: #0755 Dark Words, #0756 Light Words, #1943 Silver Metal Clip)
- Ranger (Distress Ink, Cut n' Dry foam pad)
- Mica
- Small sliding mint tin
- Ball chain
- Scissors
- Sanding block
- Crafter's Pick The Ultimate! glue
- Double stick foam tape
- Glue stick

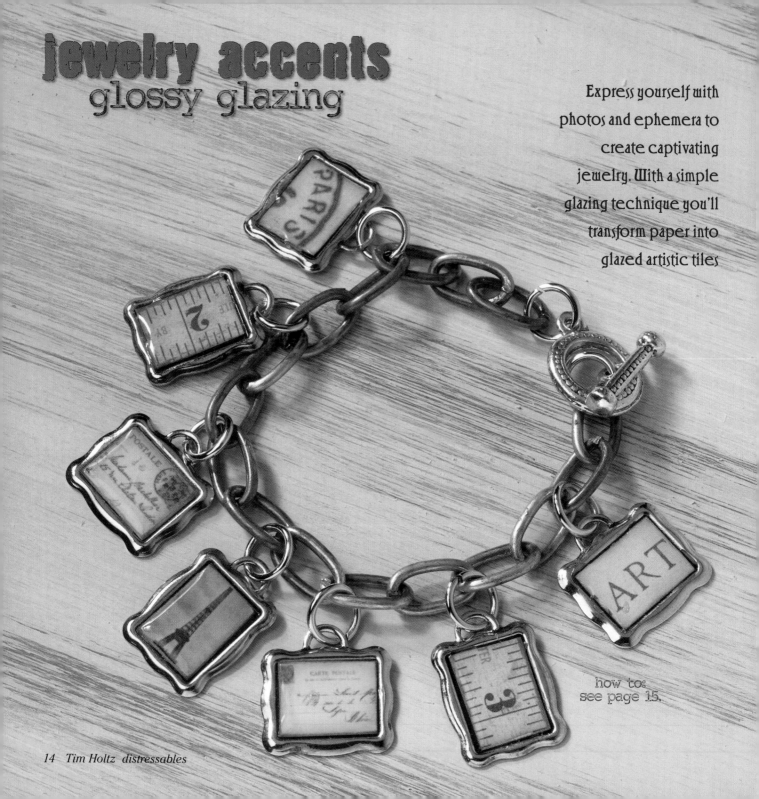

jewelry accents
glossy glazing

Express yourself with photos and ephemera to create captivating jewelry. With a simple glazing technique you'll transform paper into glazed artistic tiles

how to: see page 15.

1. Trace template on image. Cut out and ink the edges.

2. Glue into frame piece. Let dry.

3. Apply Glossy Accents to paper by outlining the edge and then filling in until the image is covered.

4. Allow Glossy Accents to dry completely. Attach to project.

Charmed Journey Bracelet
Finished size: 1" x 8"
(Shown on opposite page)

Supplies:
- Design Originals (distressables cardstock #0737 Postale, #0743 Rulers; doodads # 0754 Typewriter)
- Ranger (Distress Ink, Glossy Accents, Cut n' Dry foam pad)
- Jump rings
- Chain
- Clasp closure
- Blank frame charms
- Scissors
- Sanding block
- Crafter's Pick The Ultimate! glue

Key to My Heart Pendant
Finished size: 1 1/2"

Supplies:
- Design Originals (distressables cardstock #0742 Lock & Key; doo-dads #0752 Print Blocks, #0754 Typewriter)
- Ranger (Distress Ink, Glossy Accents, Cut n' Dry foam pad)
- Blank round pendant
- Ball chain
- Red cardstock
- Heart punch
- Scissors
- Sanding block
- Crafter's Pick The Ultimate! glue

how to: see page 15.

Keepsake Bracelet
Finished size: 5/8" x 8 1/2"

Supplies:
- Design Originals (distressables cardstock #0738 Bingo, #0737 Postale, #0743 Rulers)
- Ranger (Distress Ink, Glossy Accents, Cut n' Dry foam pad)
- Blank frame bracelet
- Scissors
- Sanding block
- Crafter's Pick The Ultimate! glue

how to: see page 15.

Print Blocks Bracelet
Finished size: 5/8" x 8 1/2"

Supplies:
- Design Originals (distressables cardstock #0743 Rulers; doo-dads #0752 Print Blocks)
- Ranger (Distress Ink, Glossy Accents, Cut n' Dry foam pad)
- Blank frame bracelet
- Scissors
- Sanding block
- Crafter's Pick The Ultimate! glue

how to: see page 15.

Use photos as well as papers for a personal keepsake.

*

Add dimensional objects to jewelry blanks and embed them in Glossy Accents.

*

Use these glazed embellishments on cards and scrapbook pages.

*

Do not heat this glaze to dry it – heat causes air bubbles in the glaze.

*

Dry objects on a level surface to allow for a smooth glazed surface.

* * *

how to: see
page 19

brilliant bottle caps
glossy glazing

Circus Time Frame
Finished size: 5" x 5"

Supplies:
- Design Originals (distress-ables paper #0748 Big Circus; Cardstock #0741 Circus, #1945 Silver Bottle Caps)
- Ranger (Distress Ink, Glossy Accents, Cut n' Dry foam pad)
- Wood frame
- Scissors
- Sanding block
- Crafter's Pick The Ultimate! glue

How to: Follow instructions on page 19 to create caps for frame. Wrap wood frame with "Big Circus" paper and glue to frame. Trim off excess. Attach bottle caps to frame when set.

1. Use a quarter as a template to trace and cut out image.

2. Glue the image inside the bottom of a cap. Let dry.

3. Fill cap with Glossy Accents starting with the edges and working into the center until the image is covered.

4. Allow Glossy Accents to dry completely. Attach to frame.

"A Cap Full of Creativity"

That's all you'll need to make extraordinary projects from an ordinary item. Discover the art of creating dimensional glazed embellishments that will have you overflowing with ideas.

Love Caps
Bracelet
Finished size: 1 1/4" x 8"

Supplies:
- Design Originals (#1945 Silver Bottle Caps; distressables cardstock #0739 Toy Blocks)
- Ranger (Distress Ink, Glossy Accents, Cut n' Dry foam pad)
- Bracelet blank
- Scissors
- Crafter's Pick The Ultimate! glue

how to:
see page 19.

Bottle Cap Buddy
Finished size: 1 1/2" x 4"

Supplies:
- Design Originals (#1945 Silver Bottle Cap; distressables cardstock #0737 Postale, #0744 Journaling; doo-dads #0756 Light Words)
- Ranger (Distress Ink, Glossy Accents, Cut n' Dry foam pad)
- 18 gauge Artistic wire
- Charms (Hand, Face, Heart)
- Eyelets   • Jump rings
- Ball chain   • Scissors
- Awl   • Sanding block
- Crafter's Pick The Ultimate! glue

How to: Follow instructions on page 19 to create cap for body. After glaze has set, pierce 5 holes in side of bottle cap using a metal awl. Cut out 2 pen nibs from Journaling cardstock and apply Glossy Accents. Let dry. Punch a hole in the end of each and attach an eyelet. Adhere doo-dad word to cap. Adhere a heart charm with The Ultimate!. Attach nibs and hand charms to cap with jump rings. Attach face charm by threading wire up through the charm and create a loop on top. Wrap excess wire and snip.

how to:
see page 19.

Enchanted Soul
Pendant or Pin
Finished size: 5" x 5 1/2"

Supplies:
- Design Originals (#1945 Silver Bottle Cap, distressables cardstock: #0743 Rulers, #0742 Lock & Key, #0737 Postale; doo-dads #0756 Light Words)
- Ranger (Distress Ink, Glossy Accents, Cut n' Dry foam pad)
- Domino
- Mica
- Charms (Wing, Crown)
- Eye hooks
- Jump rings
- Eyelets
- Pin bail
- Ball chain
- Scissors
- Crafter's Pick The Ultimate! glue
- Double stick foam tape

How to: Follow instructions on page 19 for bottle cap face. Drill 2 pilot holes on bottom end of domino. Glue cardstock to domino, then mica over cardstock using The Ultimate! glue. Trim to fit domino. Attach doo-dads words with foam tape on mica background. Cut rulers from Rulers cardstock and glue to chipboard or doo-dads header card. Sand and ink edges. Punch a hole in the end and attach an eyelet to each ruler. Screw a tiny eye hook into each drilled hole in the domino. Attach rulers to eye hooks with jump rings. Glue wing charms to back of domino. Glue bottle cap face to top of domino. Glue crown to top of bottle cap. Glue pin back to back of domino. Insert chain.

tips & tricks

Fill caps with dimensional objects (watch parts, beads, etc.) and fill with glaze.

*

Drill or poke holes in bottle caps AFTER glazing them – This will avoid any leaks of the glaze.

*

Do not heat this glaze to dry it – heat causes air bubbles in the glaze.

*

Dry objects on a level surface to allow for a smooth glazed surface.

*

Use "Dimensional Collage" technique inside caps before glazing for a creative touch to cards or scrapbook pages.

* * *

transparent illusions
transfer with tape

Layer your artistic visions with transparent images created from basic supplies. Add depth and illusion to your jewelry or paper craft projects.

Visions of Paris Pin
Finished size: 1 1/2" x 4"

Supplies:
- Design Originals (distressables cardstock #0737 Postale)
- Ranger (Distress Ink, Cut n' Dry foam pad, Glossy Accents)
- Clear packaging tape
- Clearz tilez & tabz
- Mini brads   • Foil tape
- Ringz   • Charms
- Glossy cardstock   • Scissors
- Paris stamp   • Sanding block
- Black patina (optional)

How to: Follow instructions on page 23. Edge with foil tape. Burnish with bone folder. Attach both pieces with jump rings and attach charms. Finish holes with mini brads.

Story of Life Tag
Finished size: 2 3/8" x 4 3/4"

Supplies:
- Design Originals (distressables cardstock #0743 Rulers)
- Ranger (Distress Ink, Cut n' Dry foam pad, Glossy Accents)
- Clear packaging tape
- #5 manila tag   • Paperbag Studios stamp
- Clearz tilez   • Scissors
- Mini brads   • Sanding block
- Glossy cardstock

How to: Follow instructions on page 23. Distress tag with Distress Inks. Glue rulers cardstock to tag. Attach tilez to tag with brads.

1. Apply clear packaging tape to distress-ables cardstock. Bright colors make a better transfer.

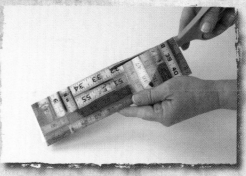

2. Burnish paper with a bone folder. Trim to size of tape.

3. Soak in warm water for 5 minutes. Begin gently rubbing off the paper with your fingers until the paper is gone. Do Not Scratch Or Rub Too Hard. Let dry.

4. Stamp an image with Black ink on White cardstock.

5. Place dried transfer over stamped image and tack with glue stick.

6. Place a tile over the image, trace and cut out. Adhere to the back of the tile with Glossy Accents.

Memoirs Box
Finished size:
1 3/4" x 5 3/8" x 7"

Supplies:

- Design Originals (distressables cardstock #0744 Journaling; #1953 Salsa Slide Mount)
- Ranger (Distress Ink, Cut n' Dry foam pad, Glossy Accents)
- Glossy cardstock
- Clear packaging tape
- Brads
- Mini brads
- Embellishments
- Wood box
- Limited Edition main stamp
- Archival ink
- Scissors
- Sanding block

How to: Follow instructions on page 23 but do not adhere transfer to tile. Place in distressed slide mount (sand and ink edges). Mat on Journaling paper. Stamp box with Archival Ink. Distress box with foam and Distress Inks. Adhere mount to mat with brads. Attach art to box with mini brads. Adhere embellishments using Glossy Accents.

Start with brighter images for transfers as the images will lighten slightly.

*

Create your own transparencies for book niches and windows.

*

Layer transparencies over photos on your scrapbook pages.

*

For larger transfers, try using laminate sheets.

*

For larger transfers, burnish with a brayer.

* * *

Through the Looking Glass
Finished size: 1 1/2"

Supplies:
- Design Originals (distressables cardstock: #0736 Library, #0740 Games)
- Ranger (Distress Ink, Cut n' Dry foam pad, Glossy Accents)
- Glossy cardstock
- Clear packaging tape
- Optical lenses
- Ball chain
- River City Rubber Works stamp
- Scissors
- Sanding block

How to: Follow instructions on page 23 but adhere transfer to lens instead of tile.

Capture your memories under glass with clever collage ideas using distressables and Memory Glass.

Believe Pin
Finished size: 1" x 3"

Supplies:
- Design Originals (distressables cardstock: #0742 Lock & Key, #0734 Print Blocks, #0743 Rulers; doo-dads #0756 Light Words)
- Ranger (Distress Ink, Cut n' Dry foam pad, Memory Glass 1x3)
- Foil tape
- Bone folder
- Black patina (optional)
- Scissors
- Sanding block

memoirs under glass
memory glass

1. Trace glass size onto distress-ables double-sided cardstock to give your art a finished back. Cut out.

2. Layer additional papers on the background and trim.

3. Cut out doo-dads. Sand and ink the edges. Glue to background.

4. Place finished piece between 2 pieces of Memory Glass. Begin applying 1/4" foil tape at the bottom.

5. Wrap foil tape around all edges, overlapping at the end. Flatten tape and burnish all edges using a bone folder. Don't press too hard or you could break the glass. Optional: Solder edges or oxidize with Black Patina.

Key to Dreams
Necklace Pendant
Finished size: 2" x 2"

Supplies:
- Design Originals (distressables cardstock: #0733 Time, #0742 Lock & Key, #0743 Rulers; doo-dads: #0751 Letter Squares, #0752 Print Blocks, #0753 Toy Blocks, #0754 Typewriter)
- Ranger (Distress Ink, Cut n' Dry foam pad, Memory Glass 2x2)
- Soldering tools (optional)
- Jump rings
- Mini key
- Ball chain
- Foil tape
- Bone folder
- Scissors
- Sanding block

how to: see page 27.

Postale Pin
Finished size: 2" x 2"

Supplies:
- Design Originals (distressables cardstock #0737 Postale; doo-dads: #0755 Dark Words, #0751 Letter Squares)
- Ranger (Distress Ink, Cut n' Dry foam pad, Memory Glass 2x2)
- Black patina (optional)
- Foil tape
- Bone folder
- Scissors
- Sanding block

Written Thoughts Pendant

Finished size: 1" x 3"

Supplies:
- Design Originals (distressables cardstock #0744 Journaling; doo-dads #0756, Light Words)
- Ranger (Distress Ink, Cut n' Dry foam pad, Memory Glass 1x3)
- Soldering tools (optional)
- Jump rings
- Pen nib
- Ball chain
- Foil tape
- Bone folder
- Scissors
- Sanding block

how to:
see page 27

Use photos or other personal memoirs by reducing the images.

*

When applying foil tape, pinch sides of tape around glass first, then flatten corners with bone folder before burnishing. This will round out the corners for a nicer look.

*

When using solder or patinas on tape, be sure to clean off any chemicals using a damp cloth with mild cleaner before wearing the art piece.

* * *

how to - see
page 31.

Numbers of Time
Hinged Canvas
Finished size: 4" x 8"

Supplies:
- Design Originals (distressables cardstock: #0733 Time, #0738 Bingo, #0734 Print Blocks, #0739 Toy Blocks; doo-dads: #0755 Dark Words, #0756 Light Words, #1943 Silver Metal Clip, #1945 Silver Bottle Cap)
- Ranger (Distress Ink, Cut n' Dry foam pad)
- Natural beeswax
- Ranger Melting Pot
- 4x4 Canvas Concepts Natural Canvas
- Hinge
- Scissors
- Sanding block
- Glossy Accents
- Embellishments
- Brush

creations
on canvas
beeswax
collage

creations on canvas
beeswax collage

1. Rub Distress pad directly onto canvas.

2. Wet a foam pad or sponge and wipe it across the inked canvas to blend and shade colors. Distress Ink reacts with water, allowing it to blend better.

3. Melt Natural Beeswax in a Melting Pot. Keep the melted wax at a constant 275 degree temp to allow you enough time to layer it.

4. Tear and cut papers for background. Brush melted wax on canvas, apply paper, and brush wax over the top of the paper. Continue until the canvas is collaged.

5. Add doo-dads and embellishments to canvas with glue.

Collage your memories on a canvas keepsake. Layer papers, photos and more with the ancient art of beeswax...

how to: see page 31.

Trinkets from Paris Canvas
Finished size: 4" x 4"

Supplies:
- Design Originals (distressables paper #0746 Big Postale; cardstock #0737 Postale; doo-dads: #0751 Letter Squares, #0754 Typewriter)
- Ranger (Distress Ink, Cut n' Dry foam pad)
- Canvas Concepts 4x4 Natural Canvas
- Naturlal beeswax
- Ranger Melting Pot
- Rusty key   • Brush
- Book plate   • Scissors
- Glossy Accents   • Sanding block

how to: see page 31.

Circus Time Canvas
Finished size: 4" x 4"

Supplies:
- Design Originals (distressables cardstock #0741 Circus; doo-dads: #0755 Dark Words, #0756 Light Words, #0751 Square Letters, #0752 Print Blocks, #0753 Toy Blocks, #0754 Typewriter)
- Ranger (Distress Ink, Cut n' Dry foam pad, Memory Glass)
- Canvas Concepts 4x4 Natural Canvas
- Naturlal beeswax
- Ranger Melting Pot
- Foil tape   • Embellishments
- Brush   • Scissors
- Glossy Accents   • Sanding block

how to: see
page 31.

Be sure to keep your wax at a constant temp to allow for consistent coverage.

*

Use a heat tool to heat up the areas on your waxed canvas and press a rubber stamp into the hot wax – allow to cool and remove stamp for an intaglio look.

*

To dull a shiny image on your collage, apply a thin layer of wax.

*

To give the wax an aged look, apply Distress Ink to cooled waxed canvas.

* * *

Life's Moments Canvas
Finished size: 4" x 4"

Supplies:
- Design Originals (distressables cardstock #0743 Rulers; doo-dads: #0751 Square Letters, #0752 Print Blocks, #0753 Toy Blocks, #0754 Typewriter, #1944 Silver Wire Clips)
- Ranger (Distress Ink, Cut n' Dry foam pad, Memory Glass)
- Studios Blackbird Mini magnifying glass
- Canvas Concepts 4x4 Natural Canvas
- Naturlal beeswax
- Ranger Melting Pot
- Foil tape
- Brush
- Glossy Accents
- Foam board
- Scissors
- Sanding block

How to: Follow instructions on page 31. Cut additional ruler from cardstock and adhere to cut piece of foam board. Attach clips to end. Glue to board, glass, and magnifying glass to canvas.

thinking outside the tag
techniques

Discover the fun of creating dimensional tags with distressables. Explore these one-of-a-kind art creations and a clever book made from what else???? Tags!

how to: see page 35.

Friends Voyage Tag Book
Finished size: 2 3/8" x 5 1/4"

Supplies:
- Design Originals (distressables cardstock: #0736 Library, #0740 Games, #0743 Rulers, #0735 Traveler; doo-dads: #0751 Letter Squares, #0752 Print Blocks, #0753 Toy Blocks, #0754 Typewriter; #1943 Silver Metal Clip
- Ranger (Distress Ink, Cut n' Dry foam pad, Memory Glass)
- 5 manila tags
- Photos
- Embellishments
- Bone folder
- Scissors
- Sanding block
- Crafter's Pick The Ultimate! glue

Distress Tags

1. Rub a Distress Ink pad directly onto both sides of the tag.

2. Spray inked tag with water. Distress Ink reacts with water, allowing it to blend better.

3. Let dry or heat with Heat Tool or Craft Iron. Repeat for all tags.

Create Ruler

1. Choose a ruler from distressables Ruler cardstock and cut it out.

2. Glue ruler to chipboard or use slide mounts or doo-dads header instead of chipboard. Let dry.

3. Trim ruler and cut to width of tags. Sand and ink the edges.

Assemble Book

1. Place cut ruler on the left edge of the tag (the side with no hole). Score with a bone folder.

2. Fold the tag along the score line back and forth to create a hinge. Repeat for all tags used.

3. Glue tags together on the left folded tab by stacking them on top of each other.

4. Glue ruler to the top and bottom edge of the book and clip together.

Journey Tag
Finished size: 2 1/4" x 4 3/4"

Supplies:
- Design Originals (distressables cardstock: #0734 Print Blocks, #0735 Traveler; #1945 Silver Bottle Cap)
- Ranger (Distress Ink, Cut n' Dry foam pad, Memory Glass, Glossy Accents)
- Letters (Chipboard, Rub-on, Acrylic)
- #5 manila tag • Foil tape
- Twine • Scissors
- Bone folder • Sanding block
- Crafter's Pick The Ultimate! glue

How to: Follow instructions for distressing tag on page 35. Create bottle cap map by gluing paper to top of bottle cap and seal using Glossy Accents. Cut out letter from Print Block cardstock and layer under Memory Glass. Seal with foil tape. Stamp out letter, or glue embellishment letters.

how to: see page 35

Under Lock & Key Tag
Finished size: 2 1/4" x 4 3/4"

Supplies:
- Design Originals (distressables cardstock #0742 Lock & Key; doo-dads: #0755 Dark Words, #0756 Light Words; #1949 Kraft distressables mini file folders)
- Ranger (Distress Ink, Cut n' Dry foam pad)
- #5 manila tag
- Mini brads • Dymo label maker
- Rusty key • Scissors
- Twine • Sanding block

How to: Follow instructions for distressing tag on page 35. Ink mini folder. Tear and attach paper to tag with mini brads. Fill folder with ephemera. Attach rusty key to tag.

how to: see
page 35

how to: see page 35

The Heart's Journal Tag Book
Finished size: 3 1/8" x 6 1/8"

Supplies:
- Design Originals (distressables cardstock: #0744 Journaling, #0733 Time; doo-dads: #0751 Letter Squares, #0752 Print Blocks, #0753 Toy Blocks, #0754 Typewriter; #1944 Silver Wire Clips)
- Ranger (Distress Ink, Adirondack Alcohol ink, Cut n' Dry foam pad)
- #5 manila tag
- Fibers • Scissors
- Pen nib • Sanding block
- Crafter's Pick The Ultimate! glue

How to: Follow instructions for distressing tag on page 35. Color clips with Adirondack Alcohol Inks (follow "Basic Techniques" instructions). Tie fibers to clip. Glue nib to tag.

tips & tricks

Create clever tags for packages and personalize them.

*

Create verses using doo-dads™ letters on tags and frame them as art.

*

Use tags for titles on scrapbook pages and cards.

*

Ironing tags creates a smooth surface to allow you to stamp on them.

*

Try sewing several finished tags together to create a patchwork background for scrapbook pages or book covers.

* * *

diamond book

Find out just how easy it is to construct this funky folded photo book. Tell a story with photos in this unique little book.

Chandler's Bubble Adventure

Chandler, age 3 at Nana's house blowing bubbles. Trying to catch the bubbles then blowing more bubbles and more bubbles and more bubbles.

(thanks to mom John Paul 2004)

A Trip to Nana's Diamond Fold Book
Finished size: 4 3/4" x 4 3/4"

Supplies:
- Design Originals (distressables cardstock #0739 Toy Blocks)
- Ranger (Distress Ink, Cut n' Dry foam pad)
- Text computer printed on vellum and embossed
- Scissors
- Sanding block
- Crafter's Pick The Ultimate! glue

how to: see page 39.

1. Fold paper into 4 squares by folding in half, and the half in the opposite direction, both "valley" folds.

2. Flip paper over and fold 1 diagonal. This fold is the opposite of the first two folds, a "peak" fold.

3. Fold paper into a flat square and crease with bone folder. Repeat for the number of pages you want.

4. Make sure you flip over page 2 so the folds are opposite pages 1 and 3. Glue the bottom square panel of page 1 to the top panel of page 2. Glue the top panel of page 3 to bottom panel of page 2. Repeat if needed.

5. For cover, cut chipboard 1/4" larger than folded square dimensions. Decorate with papers, inks, paints, etc. and glue to the top and bottom pages.

1. Cut paper in half.

2. Fold each strip into thirds, alternating "peak" and "valley" folds.

3. Place folded strips end to end and join together with tape on the back.

accordion book

Tuck your memories and photos inside this simple accordion book. It's the perfect place to journal your adventures in life.

4. Fold up paper like an accordion and crease with a bone folder.

Travel to Nowhere Accordion Fold Book
Finished size: 3" x 4 1/2"

Supplies:
- Design Originals (distressables cardstock: #0735 Traveler, #0734 Print Blocks; doo-dads #0751 Square Letters, #0752 Print Blocks, #1943 Silver Metal Clips)
- Ranger (Distress Ink, Cut n' Dry foam pad)
- Optical lens
- Twine   • Scissors
- Dymo label maker   • Sanding block
- Crafter's Pick The Ultimate! glue

How to: see page 40.

pocket book

Learn a simple fold to create a book of pockets without any scissors or adhesives. Tuck away all of your memories and tags in this pocket-sized book.

Pocket Full of Memories
Pocket Fold Book
Finished size: 2 1/4" x 5"

Supplies:
- Design Originals (distressables cardstock #0744 Journaling; doo-dads #0751 Letters Squares, #1944 Silver Wire Clip)
- Ranger (Distress Ink, Cut n' Dry foam pad)
- Book frame
- Nib
- Lock charm
- Scissors
- Sanding block
- Crafter's Pick The Ultimate! glue

how to: see page 43.

pocket book

1. Fold paper in quarters by folding in half. Then fold each side into the middle.

2. Fold in 1/4" from the right and left edges.

3. Fold in each corner to the first fold – Do NOT go over the fold.

4. Fold each side into the center.

5. Flip paper over and fold 1/2" down towards you from the top.

6. Fold paper in half and tuck the bottom corners into the top pocket corners.

7. Crease flat with a bone folder and fold in half to create a book.

Put a little shake in your page with the ease of slide mounts. With a little mica and some shakable stuff – you'll be shaking things up in the way you scrapbook.

Class Memories 'Shaker Box' Scrapbook Page
Finished size: 9" x 9"

Supplies:
- Design Originals (distressables cardstock: #0734 Print Blocks, #0743 Rulers; #1953 Salsa slide mount; doo-dads #0752 Print Blocks; #1944 Silver Wire Clips)
- Ranger (Distress Ink, Cut n' Dry foam pad)
- Mica
- Twine
- Photo corners
- Sanding block
- Crafter's Pick The Ultimate! glue
- Watch parts
- Metal letters
- Scissors

How to: Follow step-out instructions for shaker box on page 45 and attach to page.

shakerbox scrapbook

1. Adhere mica to the inside of a slide mount. Sand and ink the mount.

2. Trace the mount on background with a pencil.

3. Place foam tape inside of traced lines. Make a completely closed frame of tape. Build layers depending on the contents.

4. Fill with trinkets, watch parts, beads, buttons, etc.

5. Remove tape backing and press the mount on top of tape to seal the shaker.

Elements don't necessarily have to float on top of the background papers. Sometimes, tucking a section underneath can create an interesting effect.

'Timeless' Scrapbook Page
Finished size: 12" x 12"

Supplies:
- Design Originals (distressables paper #0745 Big Time; cardstock #0733 Time; #1944 Silver Wire Clips, #1945 Silver Bottle Caps)
- Ranger (Distress Ink, Cut n' Dry foam pad, Glossy Accents)
- Quickutz Paige Classic font
- Watch parts
- Jump rings
- Scissors
- Sanding block
- Eyelet twill tape

How to: Mat photo on black side of Time cardstock. Cut Big Time watch and tuck photo in. Die-cut title and glue to page. Follow step out instructions for Glossy Glazing on page 15 for watch part bottle caps. Punch hole in bottle caps with needle tool. Attach caps to twill tape with jump rings. Clip text to page. Ink page with Distress Ink.

HOW DO YOU MEASURE FRIENDSHIP?

TIM, ROBIN, ANd ZWICK jUSt
GOOFING OFF AS FRIEN...
it's MOMENtS LIKE the...
WE tREASURE THE MOS...

These papers allow you to take total control of your scrapbook layout with a large image on which to focus.

'Measuring Friendship' Scrapbook Page
Finished size: 12" x 12"

Supplies:
- Design Originals (distressables paper #0750 Big Rulers; cardstock #0743 Rulers; #1943 Silver Metal Clips)
- Ranger (Distress Ink, Cut n' Dry foam pad)
- Vellum
- Black acrylic paint
- Scissors
- Making Memories foam stamps
- Quickutz CK newsclips font
- Sanding block

How to: Stamp word on page with black paint. Die-cut letters using Rulers cardstock and glue to torn black cardstock on layout. Cut additional rulers from Rulers cardstock and attach to corners of photo. Print text on vellum and clip to page. Ink page with Distress Inks.

creative cards

Explore the shapes, sizes, and techniques from the clever cards created from distressables and doodads. The possibilities are truly endless.

A Song in My Heart Card
Finished size: 4" x 5 1/4"

Supplies:
- Design Originals (distressables cardstock #0736 Library; doo-dads #0751 Square Letters)
- Ranger (Distress Ink, Cut n' Dry foam pad, Memory Glass)
- River City Rubber Works stamp
- Foil tape
- Lace
- Metal corners
- Foam board
- Scissors
- Crafter's Pick The Ultimate! glue
- Sanding block

How to: Follow instructions for Memory Glass Collage on page 27. Cut out music book from Library paper. Glue to foam board. Attach pin to foam board. Stamp text with Distress Ink on cardstock. Embellish with metal corners. Ink edges of foam board and attach to cardstock. Tear edges and ink with Distress Ink.

1. Cut distressables double-sided cardstock in half. Fold in half to create a 4 1/2" x 4 1/2" square card.

2. Ink edges of card with foam pad.

3. Cut background mat to 3" x 3 1/2". Ink edges.

4. Sand and ink edges of a small slide mount

Mona Masterpiece Card
Finished size: 4 1/2" x 4 1/2"

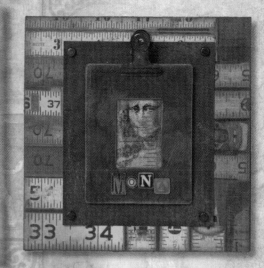

Supplies:
- Design Originals (distressables cardstock: #0743 Rulers, #0733 Time; #1954 Weathered Slide Mount; doo-dads: #0751 Square Letters, #0752 Print Blocks, #0753 Toy Blocks, #0754 Typewriter; #1943 Silver Metal Clip)
- Ranger (Distress Ink, Cut n' Dry foam pad)
- Clear packaging tape   • Mini brads
- Inkadinkado stamp   • Scissors
- Sanding block   • Crafter's Pick The Ultimate! glue

How to: Follow instructions for Tape Transfers on page 23. Adhere transfer to inside of slide mount. Embellish with doo-dads. Attach clip to slide mount. Mat with backside of Time cardstock. Cut 9x9 cardstock in half. Fold to create 4.5"x4.5" square card. Adhere collage to card. Ink edges with Distress Ink.

A Time to Remember Card
Finished size: 4 1/2" x 6"

Supplies:
- Design Originals (distressables cardstock #0733 Time; #1944 Silver Wire Clips)
- Ranger (Distress Ink, Cut n' Dry foam pad)
- Making Memories foam letter stamps
- Wordsworth stamp   • Sanding block
- Brush   • Scissors
- Acrylic paint (Black, Cream) • Mica
- Crafter's Pick The Ultimate! glue

How to: Tri-fold Time cardstock. Dry brush cream acrylic paint on inside of card. Stamp word with foam stamps and black paint on front. Stamp image with Distress and clip to inside of card. Ink edges of card with Distress Ink. Cut and adhere mica circle to watch face.

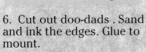

5. Adhere image inside the mount.

6. Cut out doo-dads . Sand and ink the edges. Glue to mount.

7. Place a clip on the mount. Glue a mat to the card. Glue a mount to the mat.

suppliers

Most scrapbook, rubber stamp and paper stores carry an excellent assortment of supplies. If you need something special, ask your local store to contact the following companies.

Ranger Ink – (Tim Holtz Distress Inks. Cut n' Dry Foam, Memory Glass, Glossy Accents, Melting Pot, Tim Holtz Adirondack Alcohol Inks, Blending Solution, Ink Applicator Tool, Glossy Cardstock, UTEE) www.rangerink.com

Product Performers – Pocket Watches, Mint Tins, Venture Foil Tape, 3m Foam Tape - www.productperformers.com

QuicKutz – Personal Die Cut System www.quickutz.com

Sulyn – bracelet blank, blank charms, empty pendants www.sulyn.com

Quest Beads – charms www.questbeads.com

Design Originals – distressables, doo-dads, metal accents, slide mounts, mini-file folders www.d-originals.com

Junkitz – Tim Holtz Clearz Tiles, long brads, ringz www.junkitz.com

Canvas Concepts – canvas www.canvasconcepts.com

Yaley – beeswax www.yaley.com

Tonic Studios – scissors www.kushgrip.com

Crafters Pick – The Ultimate! glue www.crafterspick.com

PM Designs – Scrapper's Sanding Block www.designsbypm.com

EK Success – Thumb Punches www.eksuccess.com

Catslife Press – rubber stamps www.harborside.com/~catslife/

Wordsworth – rubber stamps www.wordsworthstamps.com

Inkadinkado – rubber stamps www.inkadinkado.com

River City Rubber Works – rubber stamps www.rivercityrubberworks.com

PostModern Design – rubber stamps (405)-321-3176

Paperbag Studios – rubber stamps www.paperbagstudios.com

American Tag – manila tags, ball chain www.americantag.net

Lil' Davis Design – chipboard letters, bookplates www.lildavisdesign.com

Making Memories – foam stamps www.makingmemories.com

Magic Scraps – foam board www.magicscraps.com

US Artquest – mica www.usartquest.com

Many thanks to my friends for their cheerful help and wonderful ideas!
Suzanne McNeill
Kathy McMillan
Jennifer Laughlin
Angie Vangalis
Donna Kinsey
David & Donna Thomason
Lisa Vollrath
Michele Charles

Combining distressables and doo-dads to create interesting cards is so much fun, I couldn't resist adding just a few more!

Key to Friendship Card
Finished size: 3 1/2" x 4 1/2"

Supplies:
- Design Originals distressables cardstock #0742 Lock & Key
- Ranger (Distress Ink, Cut n' Dry foam pad)
- Foam board
- Mini brads
- Vellum
- Catslife Press stamp
- Rusty key
- Scissors
- Sanding block
- Crafter's Pick The Ultimate! glue

How to: Cut keyhole from cardstock and adhere to foam board. Cut out keyhole and glue in rusty key. Stamp and emboss text on vellum. Adhere to card with mini brads. Attach keyhole with mini brads. Assemble card. Ink edges with Distress Inks.

Time to Play Card
Finished size: 4 1/4" x 6 1/2"

Supplies:
- Design Originals (distressables cardstock #0738 Bingo; doo-dads: #0752 Print Blocks, #0755 Dark Words, #1945 Silver Bottle Cap)
- Ranger (Distress Ink, Cut n' Dry foam pad, Glossy Accents)
- Embossing (Ink, Powder, Heat gun)
- Word stamp
- Foam board
- Crafter's Pick The Ultimate! glue

How to: Follow instructions for Glossy Glazing Bottle Caps on page 19. Cut foam board frame and wrap with Bingo cardstock. Ink edges of frame and cardstock. Stamp and emboss text. Glue text, frame and bottle cap to card.

Enjoy the Journey...Paris Card
(photo on page 51)
Finished size: 3 1/2" x 7"

Supplies:
- Design Originals distressables paper #0746 Big Postale
- Ranger (Distress Ink, Cut n' Dry foam pad)
- Tan cardstock
- Rub on words
- Sanding block
- Foil Tape
- Crafter's Pick The Ultimate! glue
- Clearz tilez
- Twine
- Scissors
- Rusty key
- Mini brads

How to: Cut square from cardstock and cover with distressables paper, positioning postcards as desired. Cut boy from paper and adhere to cardstock. Ink edges with Distress inks. Adhere to card with mini brads. Edge tilez with foil tape. Apply rub on. Adhere to page. Tie twine around card, through key. Ink edges of card with Distress Inks.